Yanet Gonzalez is a writer and published author of spirituality, consciousness, and mysticism. She is an experienced self-growth and consciousness coach and the founder of Evolution Consulting, a coaching business she uses to create online coaching content, coaching videos, articles, newsletters, and other coaching resources for the benefit of her audience. Through her very profound, clear, sensitive, and honest prose, she addresses current challenges affecting humanity at the collective level as well as those challenges that affect individuals at a more intimate level of existence. Her writing can be described as spiritual and humanistic, which stems from a mystical dimension of life that allows her to delve into all matters related to human consciousness. Gonzalez's writing career began to bloom in late 2023 and continues to expand during the year 2024, after her life was graciously impacted by Inner Engineering, a program conducted by Sadhguru, Indian Yogi, Writer, and Mystic. The author's work is fully geared towards the wellbeing, betterment, and enlightenment of humanity, which she achieves through a profound and humanistic approach to all life.

Dedication

I dedicate this book to all living women in any part of the world and to all those who no longer grace us with their presence.

Yanet Gonzalez

IT IS NOT ABOUT LOVE

A Book of Teachings for Seekers of
Consciousness, Self-growth and Prosperity

AUSTIN MACAULEY PUBLISHERS®

LONDON * CAMBRIDGE * NEW YORK * SHARJAH

Ordering Information
Quantity sales: Special discounts are available on quantity purchases by corporations, associations, and others. For details, contact the publisher at the address below.

Publisher's Cataloging-in-Publication data
Gonzalez, Yanet
It Is Not About Love

ISBN 9798891556782 (Paperback)
ISBN 9798891556799 (ePub e-book)

Library of Congress Control Number: 2024913646

www.austinmacauley.com/us

First Published 2024
Austin Macauley Publishers LLC
40 Wall Street, 33rd Floor, Suite 3302
New York, NY 10005
USA

mail-usa@austinmacauley.com
+1 (646) 5125767

Acknowledgements

I must thank Sadhguru for his grace and for instilling in me strength, wisdom, and joy. This book would not have been possible without his teachings and example.

Table of Contents

Introduction

For nearly 300 years, my father's family has kept their roots and made their living at the same time forgotten old town of Pedroso in the province of Matanzas, Cuba. During my childhood school vacations, I along with my cousins, would find ourselves freely exploring the old town's only public cafeteria or bar, as my family still calls it, that sold the most delicious croquettes and pastries you would ever want to eat. Close to Pedroso's only cafeteria runs through an old and deserted train railway track, where way back in time, trains transported people to and from the nearby towns.

Although the railway track has not been operational for many decades, the smell of the tracks lingers in the air and permeates the town in the very early hours of the day, within a few hours of twilight, and during nighttime. It is a distinguishable and unique scent arising from the fusion of natural wood, red soil, and the steel tracks. I think of this mix as the right kind of scent any train tracks could acquire through time. For me, the abandoned railway tracks and their lingering track scent are a constant reminder of the many past rides, joyful trips, booming years, and times of prosperity that exist no more. However, I have naturally accepted the psychological nuance of the abandonment and still enjoy the train tracks with their unique and deep earthy scent.

Our perception and our reactions to past life's experiences make or destroy our existence. My purpose for this book is to address collective concerns and individual life matters and to bring light upon our true human nature and personality through a vast compilation of human themes, subjects, and topics. It is impossible to enjoy a fruitful life and lifetime if your attention is unconsciously fixed on things not for what they are but for what they provoke.

Maybe we would all have liked to stay as children forever. It was comforting, reassuring, and nurturing, plus we were jobless and taskless. However, growth and evolution cannot stay immobile. These factors are unconcerned with the human timeline; nonetheless, the process is unstoppable unless death tolls. There are only two critical points in life when it comes to time, our births and our passings.

Is it possible to control our births? No. Our parents decide how, where, and when to conceive our lives. Is it possible to control our deaths? I say, yes, it is possible. For once we take the reins of our existence in our hands, it is our sole responsibility to make sure we live and die consciously and in a decent, honorable manner.

The difference between humans and other species in the animal kingdom is that humans are now endowed with a bigger, more complex, more developed, and highly evolved thinking process and engine, which we call our brain. As humans, we capture the external world through our five senses. We collect these external impressions in the form of memory in the body. Our bodies have evolved to be able to arrange and organize these processes between the external and internal worlds with the help of the vertical column and its thousands of nerve connections to the brain and the entire body. As a species, our bodies and systems are now more organized and capable than ever before in the process of evolution, but we are failing at appreciating human evolution and the relevance of understanding ourselves.

This book and its content delve, among many other factors, upon the relevance of human evolution, the necessity of knowing ourselves deeply, and the understanding of consciousness as the only means to live a satisfying, happy, and healthy life. Life turns into an uphill battle If we do not touch the basis of our human existence and respect the foundation of our evolution and beingness. We can satisfactorily live happier, be healthier, and live inspired when we become aware of our human condition and when we understand the many self-thrown obstacles, we have placed over our shoulders by being unconscious.

This book offers the know-how to better conduct ourselves and our lives now that we have no choice but to be here. Life will no longer be an uphill battle plagued by circumstances out of our control. All the resources provided herein will make us skilled captains and rightful owners of our destinations. Isn't it true that what we deeply seek always is the successful arrival at all wanted destinations? Be it a destination where we enjoy more health, or more happiness, or better success, or having wellbeing or having more time with our loved ones or creating more and living fulfilled. This book is that opportunity to finally arrive at your intended destination.

Chapter I
The Evolved Human Being

As per the criteria of evolution, a human being must be connected and in touch with the humanity and the inner being that resides within all of us and must be additionally connected to the universe at large.

Generally, tulips count with 6 stamens arising from their pistil's base. If you happen to be observant, from time to time, you can come across some special tulips that have grown to display 7 petals or more and at least 8 stamens. But these rare findings are only visible to the eyes of those who are both attentive and curious. Ultimately, would not it be a great loss if someone is not there to notice this unique and rare tulip among the others in the bunch? It would be because for some reason this tulip has manifested a different interiority compared to the other tulips. In the gardening world, this could mean stronger and more long-lasting tulips or tulips with greater reproductive capabilities; thus, better harvesting. However, it would be for a gardener or flowering company to decide how this tulip can make their gardens or trade better. For me, the onlooker, I am left with the satisfaction that the one special tulip did not go unnoticed.

It is quite relevant for our lives to be both, naturally perceptive, and to have a different interiority. In the world of tulips, the fact that one tulip displays different characteristics may be a rare miracle of nature for that species, but when it comes to us, humans, working on our inner selves and cultivating a better interiority is now in our own hands and outside of nature's realm. Would not it make more sense for us to have a saying on how we become better or more capable human beings than to allow nature to decide this for us? This is indeed our own challenge to go through and accomplish.

Then, how do we accomplish becoming better human beings and being endowed with enhanced capabilities? It begins with one noticing, realizing, and accepting that one needs change. Only by altering our current way of life, our thinking, and our acting, we can bring change to the table. Creating a plan for change is the first step to enhancing our inner selves and enhancing our lives. Just thinking about the need for change without effectively going after at least one way in which change can come is a waste of mental energy. If you internally realize and feel that something in you requires change, that is the moment to seek change and not lose the momentum. We know that our daily lives have a way to separate us from what we seek internally, but we must persevere and persist in this seeking.

If you happen to be somewhat in touch with yourself, it would be quite easy to determine in which ways you can seek change for your betterment.

What does it mean to be in touch with our inner selves? Our interactions with the external world have rendered it almost impossible to have a relationship with who we are internally. Right now, all the interactions that take place in our awareness are related to what we have become in relation to the external world, and the relationship with our inner selves is no longer viable.

For instance, the fact that we bare first names and surnames, the fact that we are from a specific part of the world, or the fact that we have identified with what we do for a living, plus the identifications with our professional careers and educational degrees, all of these have become all we know about who we are, but these things are not what we are. These things speak only of our correlation with the external world and have become things that we have had to acquire to conform to social belonging, to satisfy economic needs, and due to cultural demands, among other socio-economic needs.

Then, if since our childhoods, all the attention has unequivocally and unilaterally been conditioned to satisfy our needs within the frame of the external world, is it possible that all we are in the present moment is a collection of information, words, and impressions? Absolutely.

This is a phenomenon I call "World or External Conditioning" and it crisscrosses many areas from our childhood upbringing, which trespasses into our current state of personal affairs.

In other simpler words, this is a phenomenon where you cease to be *You* to become someone that can deal with and belong to the outer world. In any event, is it not the relationship with the external world and our adaptation that brings better chances at survival? In a purely animalistic way, yes, but we are now an advanced species. We are now at the top of the evolutionary ladder, and we have a choice to follow our animal instincts or to find a way to bring forth our best understanding of this process of evolution for our betterment. Nothing in our evolution dictates or instigates a separation from ourselves in order to survive in the world. On the contrary, we are sufficiently evolved to know that if we remain true to our beingness we can achieve a more plentiful way to survive and thrive in the external world.

By looking at the state of the world today, you will agree that approaching the external world in purely animalistic and unconscious ways has brought about disease, over consumption, the annihilation of whole natural and animal systems, human annihilation, and has brought much detriment in the form of mental illnesses, anxiety, depression, and other host of mental and physical imbalances. The number of illnesses our ancestors suffered in their time pales in comparison to the host of thousands of illnesses that are being suffered today. It is as though all the advances we have progressively made have deteriorated our lives and existence in a profound way. This has come because we are not acting from our inner selves but from external conditioning. This is not a fair or sound way of life.

For individual reasons, it is extremely important that we re-establish the connection to our beingness. However, this connection also poses great relevance at a collective and at a human level. The moment we re-establish this lost connection, we will be successful at achieving our individual goals, and we will be able to satiate our needs and act in the world not from world conditioning but from our interiority. This is the only type of action that has proven to bring both honor and satisfaction at an individual level and honor and satisfaction to the world at large.

The process of getting to know one's interiority is rather uncomplicated but requires commitment and understanding. This connection back to us is the foundation of human equality, self-respect, and respect for all life on this planet. Many atrocities are being committed daily as we continue to act just toward our individual gain, or we continue fostering impossible profits for larger groups, corporations, or other entities to the dismaying detriment of our planet.

Until we become resolute and unwavering in finding the connection to our inner selves, the way of approaching our prosperity on the planet will always be to the detriment of others and to the detriment of ourselves in the long run. In the same way that you are acting just on your behalf, many others are out there effectively doing the same. This way of acting in the world is both unconscious and unsustainable, bringing only brief moments of material satisfaction to us and generally a great deal of suffering to others as we pursue more and more material gain. We could enjoy all the comfort the world can provide and live as conveniently as queens and kings live. However, if our satisfaction is only temporary, we are still acting from world conditioning and have become a destructive force. The choice is ours to act from our inner selves and beingness and use only what is necessary for our survival or continue acting from world conditioning and become a force that is always destructive, unsatisfied, unconscious, and able to attract illnesses, disease, and unhappiness.

Chapter II
The Human Perception

A few years ago, in one of his video talks, Sadhguru mentioned a trip he made to Lebanon where he visited the homeland of poet Kahlil Gibran, best known as the author of The Prophet. Far from the qualification of an avid reader, the story of this poet caught my attention, so I decided to purchase the book upon having some extra time.

Shortly after having seen Sadhguru's video, an image of what appeared to be a book came to my mind during a meditation. The image was of a very ancient golden sailboat all by itself against a pitch-black background. I did not recognize this image from anything I had ever seen before.

One day, while having some time in my hands, I sat down to purchase the book written by Kahlil Gibran, the poet Sadhguru had talked about. I keyed in the title of the book and to my surprise, there it was, the exact same image as I had seen it in my meditation. The image in my earlier meditation had revealed to me what I was going to encounter a few days later: an original edition of The Prophet made in America in 2021, which portrayed an ancient golden sailboat against a pitch-black paperback cover.

The incident above described is just a part of many other bits and pieces constituting what I understand as the flourishing of my perception.

Then, it begs the question to ask: What is Human Perception?

However, even if I could provide a properly defined answer to this question, it would not get us near to understanding what it is. Because perception is not a phenomenon that one can narrow down to a few words in our vocabulary, providing a concise definition of what perception is would not even begin to cover what it truly is.

Human perception is not bound by descriptive content but by human connection.

If you recall, in my previous chapter, "The Evolved Human Being", I discussed how straightening up our connections with our inner being, with the world at large, and with the universe made us evolved and able to touch our humanity, this is a pre-requisite for becoming perceptive. If there is no connectivity with our inner beings or with all that surrounds us, it is not possible for a human to experience perception or to know what it is or what it is for.

Sometimes life's circumstances demand great efforts and great sacrifices from us on a daily basis. When perception opens for us, it is easier to navigate these efforts, which can effectively become also joyful to accommodate.

Think of Khalil Gibran's sailboat bound by the roughness of the winds and the high seas versus today's mightier ships. The first, being a sailboat, counts with numerous sails and the expertise of the sailors and its captain to command it to its destination. However, made of wood, is fragile and easily distracted from its course.

The latter is a self-propelled iron and steel welded vessel with pre-planned positioning, no sails, and no sailors to save the boat. By being very sturdy, these vessels are no longer fragile or easily sinkable.

Now, you can think of Khalil Gibran's sailboat as a human being who has surrendered to perception and now counts with extra help to get where it needs to go. The captain, the sailors, the wind, the seas, the Sun, the sails, the seagulls, the northern star, the vessel itself, and even magical mermaids will ensure one gets to where one needs to go. Suddenly, the fragile sailboat made of wood is not fragile anymore. By historical events, did not the

Titanic sink to the bottom of the cold ocean? So, it is not just about the vessel, it is also about how well perceived and crafted the arrival is.

Then, the functionality of our perception is to ensure that we get safely and sound to our intended destinations while enjoying the journey.

Perception guides us in our journeys of Life. From pre-planning to executing, it is there along the line, guiding each of our steps and helping us avoid mistakes. Perception also clears our paths and suggests ways we can walk upon them.

Think of Perception as an inner compass that is bound not by imaginary longitudes and latitudes or even by the geomagnetic north but by the True North.

Chapter III
The Human Creativity

There exists a way in which we could understand much more about our lives and about our own existence if we made use of Astrology for the true relevance and significance it proclaims over our destinies.

If you have ever read a horoscope for yourself or others, you might be aware of those generalized traits ascribed to a Taurus sun sign. Their horoscope readings usually describe that such sun signs, among other things, will be very drawn to music, beauty, and all sorts of artistic genres giving them the ability to create through these forms of art. Born as a Taurus myself, however, this is a concept that has been very far from my own personal experience.

Indeed, for decades, I felt that I lacked creativity. I did not feel like a creative person. I was not used to creating anything with my own two hands. After all, I was not even inclined to pursue or deeply admire anything related to the arts and the music worlds. I had no intent to create through such art mediums and the fact that I have Venus as the sole dispositor of my chart never helped me develop any forms of art either. Venus could have made me a great lover of the arts or a great artist, but that is not what happened to me.

However, the whole confusion with my creativity was clarified as soon as my perception opened. Since this happened, I can now access, enjoy, and develop all sorts of creations, plus create easily without restrictions.

Creativity is not attached just to those who paint, make music, or do art. We are also creating when we bring to life any new forms with our bare hands.

By all accounts, nature is our greatest creator and greatest teacher of natural creativity. For me, this type of natural creativity and example is the one that I would finally be drawn to and stay happy to explore.

Undoubtedly, we can create new things by means of our own jobs and professions. However, these forms of creation tend to arise attached to stress, subject to time constraints, and are made to fulfill otherworldly human needs. As such, I do not see this as pure human creativity.

True Human Creativity arises from within each of us and is unique to each of us. We don't learn it through books or through already established forms; thus, it is free from distortions. That which we conceive and create cannot be copied or simulated by others. This is a form of creativity that now only we understand and only we can conceive, develop, and maintain. Think for a moment of a baby being conceived and nurtured by a mother. Now another woman comes and desires to copy, develop, and maintain within her own body this very same baby. No such thing is possible.

There is a large body of evidence to support why humans should strive to tap into this form of innate human creativity. For once, the individual creator rejoices in these creations, and these creations will never harm others or bring inequalities. This new way of creation brings us health, joy, wellbeing, happiness, and opportunities. What we create with our own very hands will bring health and well-being to ourselves and to our families. So, the value of the output of the creation is as worthy as the value of the input.

If we scan the world around us, it is easy to see that for many decades humans have failed to develop themselves and their world in the most conscious, equitable, and sustainable way. Social inequalities abound and where whole communities have access to water and sewer, many others drink water from rain ponds and pile their feces up amidst their own places of abode. However, in both cases, people continue to suffer from illnesses, malaise, and diseases. Western world's populations are as sick as the people living in less favored geographical locations. The illnesses and the diseases are there, it is just about the source of these being different. Then, we are living very comfortably compared to decades ago, but we are not happier or healthier and we are definitely not enjoying our lives.

If we can create our personal worlds and our societies from this inner, perceptive, and conscious way of creation, there will be no place for inequalities or unsustainability.

When we create unconsciously, we know what we are creating, but we don't know what we are destroying. In this way, humans are building the world today and it can be changed by adopting this new way of human creativity that can empower us individually and empower the world at large in a completely different way where collaboration, cooperation, union, and consciousness thrive.

This human creativity arising from our inner beings, perception, and the inner creative source is one that is different and novel, plus is always humane and decent. It will provide us with what we need to live well and be happy. Remarkably, this is the best way in which we can support ourselves while becoming a source of wellbeing for the world at large.

Chapter IV
The Human Health
and Wellbeing

No human success can ever depart from a point of unwellness. Our primary point of success is not about money, resources, careers, or other external factors. Health is our primary point of success. Unfortunately, we have made everything outside ourselves the benchmark for achievement. It is neither possible nor sustainable for the human body to act in the world and take care of the many activities we take part in and still maintain physical or mental integrity.

Our physicality and mind are not built on iron and steel like a statue. Our bodies are made of complex systems that need rest, health, maintenance, and wellbeing to keep strong and in good condition. We have forgone the importance of looking after our health and have fallen victim to a myriad of illnesses and diseases that are crippling us daily. We go out there to make a living and want to make some wealth but undermine ourselves in this process. It is a crime to sustain the body's functions by popping pain killers and ingesting artificial energy drinks.

The most glorious and amazing things we have are our bodies and our minds, but the pressure we are putting on both to sustain our lives and survive is not reasonable.

Today or for the past 20 years and going in crescendo, we have had to become slaves to the new and emerging technologies. The use of computers, keyboards, cellphones, computer mice, etc., is making us suffer a host of diseases that affect our hands, fingers, muscles, tendons, eyesight, and whole bodies. We go ahead and name these affections to give them a name in the medical encyclopedia and then to be able to prescribe pills for pain management, but the bottom line is that carpal tunnel syndrome happens in your hand and involves your whole arm from hand to shoulder including the median nerve. This type of affection has come from repetitive use of the mouse and keyboard and the hand not being able to keep its health. Once we have an illness, a disease, or once our bodies don't work well what does it matter what the affection is called? Anytime our bodies are not working well the only ones benefiting from our affections are the medical doctors. We can't make use of our bodies any more in an integral and healthy way.

If we don't become life-sensitive and if we don't respect and cherish our bodies, we will live a lifetime of seeing doctors and taking pills, and getting behind on our progress. Being unhealthy or artificially sustained is the same as walking half dead and half alive. It is not that it matters when we depart from this planet. But would not you live better and prefer to feel happy, healthy, joyful, and fulfilled? I am sure the answer is yes. And, if the answer is no, then you are already gone. There is no point for you to live this life here on this planet and take space.

Health is and should be our primary point for all else we do in life. Whether we do a lot or we do very little in terms of our actions in the world, our health and well-being should be intact and always vibrant.

Today's mental health is a very worrisome topic. Depression has for very long existed, and we have successfully found ways to take people out of depressive states. But there is a new host of mental affections like anxiety, panic attacks, suicidal behavior, mental stress, bipolar behavior, and many other mental health issues that have emerged and are taking control of people's minds from very young ages.

The problem is coming from not realizing that our physical bodies, minds, and emotions work in tandem and are connected to each other. If our heads would not be tied up to the rest of the body by the neck, then you can say the brain works on its own accord and has distinctive and separate functions and we can call all mental illnesses a brain problem. However, this is not how the body works.

We have failed to realize how intertwined our system is within and something that hurts in your arm can have an effect and hurt also in your neck area. But we have learned through science that dissecting and separating is better than looking for the whole and maintaining integrity. This is why we are at this moment in history where we know all about the most miniscule particles and know how each cell in the body works within its system, but we can't see how this same cell has a way of affecting a distant part of the body. And those illnesses that take our bodies hostage such as fibromyalgia, which is a generalized nerve pain problem that involves many systems within the body, these types of affections remain as ghost illnesses as medical doctors and science can't explain them. Many of these generalized illnesses are categorized as the patients' mind playing tricks on them. Way to go, right?

However, it is not science or medicine's job that our bodies are healthy and well-kept. That is our job.

The body, the mind, our chemistry or emotions, and our energies make who we have been since birth. It is not possible for a human being to function well if all these systems are not connected and if we don't function from them in union.

Energy is behind everything that moves and grows. A baby will develop well if there are womb nutrients and if there exists a proper amount of energy behind the growth of every system that is forming. Otherwise, growth stunts. While we are not babies any longer, still energy is behind each move we make and behind the proper maintenance of our systems and cellular growth. It is for us to maintain the health of our energy system so that we can be blessed with well-being and health.

The only way to achieve and maintain health and well-being is first by being aware that we are not made as machines and that our bodies need our attention and care each day and second to truly incorporate in our understanding that to live well, we need to see our bodies for the unified system that it is. Only then we will enjoy health, wellbeing, and live a happy life.

Chapter V
The Human Condition

Our mothers would have been very worried about our condition had we not crossed our baby years' milestones with flying colors. However, we grow up and spend the entirety of our lives behind a desk doing the same functions day in and day out not realizing that our existence is consumed with monotonous tasks cutting out any possibility of further human milestones.

Notwithstanding, we like security and reliability in our acquired skills and abilities for after all our survival depends on this.

So, in the name of survival, we are going about our lives in a most enslaving and encapsulated way of acting. No wonder our sense of freedom is so limited. Feeling very trapped inside only comes to light in exceptional moments of suffering and distress. This is our current human condition. One in which we feel trapped and unable to realize ourselves. We could say that while we attempt or succeed at external growth, still within we are unable to move an inch forward in our inner well-being.

This has come because we have mistaken inner well-being with external comfort.

To change today's human condition, we need to begin by physically and mentally experiencing happiness, health, joy, and well-being first. If we keep attempting to get to happiness, health, joy, and well-being through the acquisition of material things or materialism we will reach illnesses and diseases and will never be well.

The solution to survival is not to pile up insurmountable amounts of stress but to do our work and activities through health, peace, joy, and wellbeing.

The stress phenomenon is a trademark of Western countries and particularly of the United States. It is an all-inclusive term to memorialize the ways in which we conduct business and life here. All our activities are being conducted in some form of fast pace, yet with great exigence towards attention to detail. To make matters worse, technology has come to stay and make stress more pervasive and damaging. Stress is just a synonym of dehumanization for humans are assets that serve to enhance the profits of a multitude of entities and corporations for the promise to maintain your own livelihood. Yet, your own life, health, and wellbeing are at stake.

Then can we solve the stress issue? Or could we solve how to respond to stress?

We can't possibly solve the stress issue as this is not directedly related to our behavior but to how capitalism behaves. Capitalism is not a friend of humans. Capitalism is only friends with money and profits. Specifically, shareholder capitalism has brought half of America's diseases to the people. The unconscious and uncontrollable capitalistic ways of pursuing money and the sociopathic approach to enrichment have no mercy on the people. Each financial system including mortgage lending, mortgage servicing, reverse mortgages, bank loans, credit card usage, student loans, car loans, financing, re-financing, private loans, investments, federal interest rates, and credit scores systems, all have emerged to control our hard-earned money, our assets, our growth, our lives, and what progress we ultimately can make.

All these systems of finance and lending have come to support the high pricing of all main products we need for our sustenance. Now we are left picking up the pieces while they fatten their pockets and vaults. There are more decent and more humane ways to make a decent living that do not entail savaging each other.

Then, could we solve how to respond to stress? Yes, this is the only tool in our hands.

We must learn to modify our human condition by ceasing to act as mere spectators and sufferers of stress and human abuse. We must be more involved in everything that restricts us in our progress and fight against those things, people, and systems that foster unwarranted social and individual stress.

We need to step up to our game and become better human beings. We need to stop living so individualistically and so focused on only our problems. The system is turning a blind eye and being abusive in the same fashion that we are turning a blind eye to each other and being abusive toward each other. People make the systems and then the systems perpetuate themselves.

Our acquired and sustained individualism has come from the separation evolution graciously allotted us; however, being a double sword, we have not learned to use the knife wisely and are now cutting ourselves and others. If we were able to use this separation from all else not as a self-defeating aspiration but as a complimentary addition to what we are, we could graciously walk this planet doing the greatest benefits to others and in the process would benefit ourselves. The idea of perceiving a separation was for us as humans to evolve better and faster than other species, but that is not what has taken place. We have effectively taken over the world as to tools use and implementation, plus the ability to utter sounds that are somehow structured, but that's it. In the end, we have not been able to grasp the grandiosity of evolution and have undoubtedly stepped on our own toes.

If we continue encapsulated with the myriad of activities that the world offers, and we don't pay attention to our systems, leaders, and communities, we can be taken advantage of for longer than it took us to evolve to this point. The point of being the most advanced species on the planet is not a matter of comparing with other four-legged non-speaking species, but to understand how this advantage can become humanity's foundation to live better than animals living in the jungle and to avoid crimes against humanity. By all accounts our cities could look clean of everything, including homelessness; yet our jungles feel better to animals than our own cities feel to us. Our separation from nature has stripped us of the most basic traits of compassion, care, and duty to care for others. Animals at large don't destroy their environment; we are the only animals that destroy our own environments and ecosystems.

Humanity needs to live up to the expectation of real advancement that evolution has provided. And again, this is not a matter of comparing to other species, this is a matter of understanding that we need to become better humans every day. We need to act with compassion and understanding towards others and with no animosity. The fact that our inner humanity can't transpire and can't even permeate our human interactions demonstrates that we have not lived up to our evolution but only to the egotistic traits separation from nature has brought.

Chapter VI
The Human Awareness

Being medicated and controlling pain through barbiturates do effectively hide our physical pain.

Yet, the pain is very much there still, only dormant until the next dose.

Why do we hide the pain instead of feeling the pain?

If we opt to feel the pain, we could get to the bottom of our ailments or affections. We can then treat the problem from its roots and not just ease the condition. But, if we numb de pain, we no longer have an accurate assessment of how sick we are. Pain and discomfort are not there to bother us. The body mounts these responses to let us know that something is not quite well, and we need to know about it. But we tame the pain, and we believe we are fine, and we go about our daily lives. So, we shut down our own intelligence because we can't deal with paying the necessary attention right away and thus disrespect our own signs.

It takes human awareness to distinguish between effective healing and masquerading the pain. It takes human awareness to make the right choice. But we need to begin by understanding and having a recognition that we are talking about our own bodies. How is this not of extreme importance? It will be of extreme importance to someone whose awareness has flourished. Recognizing the sanctity of our bodies is one of the first signs that we live in awareness and have become less ignorant.

Awareness begins with the realization that we are more than flesh and bones. It opens our inner intelligence to let us see that there are many things in between. Once we realize that there is more past the human physicality then we begin accepting and respecting our bodies in a proper and conducive manner.

When awareness of our own human bodies flourishes, we start being more patient with ourselves, more respectful, more compassionate, and more attentive. We will then never again hide the pain. If we feel pain, we will pay the necessary attention and deal with it consciously and proactively. After all, are not these bodies the only companions we have for the entirety of our lives? We ought to love the body and be there when it needs us to be.

Becoming aware will progressively make us realize how unfair we have been to ourselves. Ultimately, if we mistreat our own bodies, which are the basis of our existence, could not we be unfair also to ourselves in many other areas? Definitely.

Awareness begins at the foundation of our lives: our bodies. Once we profoundly love and respect our bodies and become one with them, this union will bring truths of existence that could not be revealed to us otherwise. Through awareness, we will be endowed with the workings of this body and life. It will be like getting to know minutiae that only now that we are interested, we get to know. And we will begin understanding more and more about ourselves and human life.

Awareness will reveal, clarify, and set the right path for us. Think of a continuous and great Aha moment happening while we conduct our daily lives.

Awareness seeps through when we pierce the veil of our unconsciousness and ignorance. Once it sets in, it is a graceful companion for life. Think of awareness as the way in which your whole body responds in appreciation of your nurturing efforts. Life is sensitive and we should be too.

All that there is to know, understand, and see about life and the world around us becomes clear once we act in awareness and once our consciousness develops. Awareness allows us to place ourselves in the most suitable situations so that our lives don't feel dragging and out of control. If our awareness flourishes, we will be able to conduct our lives with great attention to detail and focus. Unawareness brings a lack of focus, concentration, and lack of steadiness in our actions. If we want to know the significance of past, present, and future, we need to become aware and able to discriminate even how the passage of time affects our expectations and achievements. By living with mixed past experiences guiding our present and future it becomes difficult to cross over barriers that we need to cross to get to any type of success in our lives. We seek success continuously; however, any type of success not achieved through awareness is short-lived and very hard to maintain.

Throughout time, both, our human bodies, and our lives have gone through intense evolutionary and existential detailing, polishing, and evolution, and all this wisdom is contained within the boundaries of our physicality. Unless we break the self-barriers that deny us access to such wisdom, we will find it difficult to become objects of our development and shall forever remain subject to insensitivity and negation.

Negating our own awareness and evolution perpetuates life stagnation and physical disease.

Chapter VII
The Human Growth

We must not stay little in body or in mental faculties. Our cells are prepared for growth and expansion. They have been doing their jobs for thousands of years and know what to do and how to do it well. If we stay in good health and well-being, then nothing can halt our human growth. The idea of being birthed is to go from baby to adult while we experience life and learn about its ups and downs.

However, our tendency to live in the past and go blindly gliding through the present is an example of staying little. Many of our present difficulties reflect past childhood traumas or impressions. These impressions embedded in our memory remain trapped and without a place to go. Anytime a present situation arises that is similar to a past negative experience our mind takes us back to the memory of the past impression. This constant resurgence of negative impressions wreaks havoc on our emotions and mental stability.

The mind is constantly making memories of everything we experience in the external world. It also makes memories of our internal responses to the environment including experiences with other people. It does this as a method of self-preservation while it learns from the environment, which is the only way to self-preservation. Thus, this is the way life has developed itself and will continue to do so. We have the capacity to understand this and should know well how we respond to these exuberant and constant traits of adaptation, evolution, and development.

Our lives are incredibly sensitive and smart, and we should strive to make the most sensical decisions when it comes to our reactions and responses to our environment.

Does this mean that we need to deny and believe that we have not gone through discomfort, pain, or trauma while making it to our adulthoods? No. But, we do need to understand this life well to be able to overcome strong negative impressions of the past so that we don't live in opposition with ourselves and with others.

The more we grow as humans, the better lives we will experience. Should you rather keep returning to hurt and discomfort or overcome it and never again think about it or feel disgraced about it? That is all growth means and it needs to happen within each of us because those bothering memories and sentiments are only within the realm of the sufferer. I can sympathize with your pain, but I can't feel it for you. So, this is an individual task.

Human growth means upgrading our present condition of pain, sorrow, and past negative experiences to a present time that we can enjoy.

After all, had the past been a good experience, you would have no contradictions with it. We need to seek this balance of mind and emotions where past memories do not hijack the present memories.

The only way in which we can determine our own future is by not allowing the past to interfere with what we want now. We may have not wanted those things that took place in the past; however, they happened anyway. But now, it is in our control to ensure they don't repeat. And especially that they don't repeat in our own minds and emotions. Right now, if you do think of any negative things, they will still come with the same intense disgust they happened in the past, meaning that we are re-living things over and over. The bottom line being that nothing negative in the past should be a part of a new life experience or a part of our future. We should grow our old problems and dismays to be able to evolve into more balanced human beings.

It is also certain that all our current life's decisions, from small to very relevant, are made based on the past that we have lived and on all accumulated past experiences. We can only imagine the many unwarranted limitations we have imposed upon ourselves by living this way.

It is possible to allow the past to rest if we work hard now in our human growth and personal development. In this way, we can be free to choose a better present for us while building a more suitable future.

Human growth is the solution to most human suffering.

Chapter VIII
The Human Transcendence

At any given time, we have all experienced employers with zero humanity within, as well as employers who are extraordinary. It is our encounters with those employers that lack humanity the same that come to shape the landscape for deeper questions into our human condition. When it comes to the workplace, a lack of humanity can come in many shapes and forms. It could manifest, for example, in the employers' inability to be compassionate and understanding towards employees. It also manifests when employers refuse to accommodate employees' needs and even when they assume cunning positions to deceive employees and exploit them past their reasonable capacities.

Then, one poses the question of what has overcome their humanity, or one might also ask, was there any humanity within these individuals after all?

Taking into consideration many possible variants, one must conclude that these employers never had any humanity within because nothing at all can obscure our humanity, nothing. Money can't obscure our humanity. Fame can't obscure our humanity. Possessions and wealth can't obscure our humanity. Our personal philosophies can't obscure our humanity. Poverty, illiteracy, and underdevelopment can't obscure our humanity.

So, if neither money nor poverty can obscure our humanity what could? And the answer is that only we do that to ourselves.

However, how could a human being lose the humanity within? We will get to this part, but before it begs to analyze how most businesses get empowered today.

How does wealth acquisition take place? A business gets set up and through the implementation of processes and procedures, it begins to grow. After a few years, and most likely without any tangible benefit to employees, the business begins to leave a profit which allows the owners to acquire more business ventures. By this stage, personal assets have probably tripled, and these individuals/owners could very well already own the assets to live the rest of their lives comfortably, while effectively also ensuring that family wealth can last for several generations.

However, money, fame, wealth, and status can become a double sword. The seeking of more wealth acquisition is now a mental want and a need as these individuals no longer accept a possible stumble and fall from fame and status, which drives them to human exploitation. This exploitation is not only of employees but of the resources in their communities. So, it all begins with a small business that consolidates then expands and branches out. This branching out does not necessarily mean expanding the initial business concept. This is a stage of capital acquisition regardless of the initial business mission.

All the above would be alright and acceptable if the seeking for more and more wealth was not disparaging, or unnecessary and if inventory and resources were not limited.

Would not it be a more sensible and more humane position to either stop accumulating wealth or have a plan to build additional wealth over long periods of time and give others a fair share now? It would be, but this is not what is happening. We are not building wealth according to our current necessities or to cover this lifetime's survival. The wealth being built is merely for future capital acquisition and accumulation. This is predatory, inhumane, disrespectful, selfish, and unfair to this generation of people now. Why hide a mountain of bread when thousands have none?

Then, how could a human being lose the humanity within? Our humanity is not tradeable. We can't trade our humanity for money, fame, wealth, status, or possessions. So, these employers who show a lack of compassion for their employees, trick them, and squeeze them for more money, have never been touched by their own humanity.

Neither having money nor the lack thereof will change this fact.

Transcending the limitations of inhumanity should be in the business agendas of many today. We can pretend to be fair at this business game, while we surreptitiously amass possessions, damage, and dispose of others along the way. However, this is only for our spirit to know.

Chapter IX
The Human and
the Environment

How we live and die not knowing this Earth that we walk upon can be the subject of a whole new book.

I have seen Earth being called by other such names as dirt, mud, and the like. The fact that we relate the soil that we walk upon to mud or dirt shows our disdain and lack of compassion for the very source of our existence.

No wonder then we are so separate from our inner beings and humanity. No wonder then the disregard for the compulsive consumption and materialistic approach to everything. Knowing this Earth does not mean locating where countries are and identifying the names of world capitals. Knowing Earth means understanding the origins of our evolution and maximizing our capacity for equitable survival.

There are thousands of books describing flowers, trees, seeds, and nature. However, we barely spend any time taking care of or enjoying the grace of nature and creation. Thus, a question naturally arises, why so much knowledge? What is the purpose of facts, data, and categorization? It just feels as if the more data we collect the further we are from solid ground. Is it that our sense of wonder dissipates once we are presented with those key facts that we should have explored on our own? Is it that so much science speculation has left us dried out and uninterested? This is an open-ended question.

The fact of the matter is that as humans we have very little desire to be in contact with our environment and with nature. There might be some earth regions where there is still interest in nature and the planet, but in overall humans have placed themselves as far from nature as they possibly can. Not far in terms of location, far in terms of having the planet and nature in their hearts and as part of their conception of this life.

Every meal we consume is wholesomely made from soil and its nutrients. There is nothing we eat either fresh or artificially made that does not come from this soil and from this planet. Even the grossest foods and materials we use, eat, or consume today are all from this planet and all dug up from our soil.

The thousands of plastics used in households and by consumers at large and the tons of metal used for all technology from cellphones to sky satellites are coming from earth's soil, minerals, metals, and crystals. Nothing we see, eat, or hold in our hands has yet come from outer space. Effectively only pieces of meteors have crossed Earth's atmosphere, and it has not been for the good of the vegetation and animal life then in the existence.

Whether we see this planet or not as an endless pit of resources depends on how conscious we are of its existence and our relationship to it. We are a part of this Earth's ecosystems just as insects and plants are. We affect other species and other inhabitants of this planet when we misunderstand our gross usage and our continued misuse. Each ecosystem has developed alongside others, and they depend on each other for survival. We are the only members of an ecosystem that do not want to live in peace, harmony, and cooperation with anything else. We over consume and pile up and then throw away and forget. We forget that we still use and need for survival the same systems we are destroying. Each plant and animal out there cohabiting with us today reproduces, lives, and dies in a more conscious, decent, and becoming manner than we ever have. That is to say, the animals and plants we have so far left with some life.

How things that are rooted and can't move or how things that move but can't think can act and behave better than us is a matter of great sadness. Our evolution has put us in a place and time where we should be the ones taking care, loving, nurturing, and protecting those things more vulnerable. Yet, we have taken it upon ourselves to forfeit this job to those and those things less evolved and more vulnerable. Bees, insects, plants, and trees have done more for our health than we have done for their benefit.

We have no regard for the grace of our evolution or for the fate of humanity. Many of us occupy much more space than we need and are consuming what others should be consuming and having.

The recognition of this Earth as our mother and sustaining force and the conscious use of the existing resources should be a primary seeking and understanding. The only way one loves a mother is if she has been nurturing and caring exactly as this Earth has been towards humanity. Yet, we underestimate the relevance of this love and protection and savage her. No wonder, we savage, mistreat, and hurt each other as well.

If we expect to last long as a human race, it is obligatory that we consider understanding deeply what this planet offers and understanding the rules of creation when it comes to sharing and preserving. No one in any part of this Earth should have more rights than another from a different location. We all have the right to survive well when it comes to basic survival, i.e., eating, dressing, having access to water and shelter, and receiving education or making a living. Appropriation of resources for the sake of piling up capital is not reasonable or humane and should not be allowed in any place under Earth's dome.

That humanity has lived eras of imperialism, conquests, religious conversions, extermination of whole races and other sanguinary human exploitations does not mean we need to continue behaving as barbaric or need to continue repeating history.

Being in connection with Earth, with nature, and with ourselves is the only way to respect the planet and its people.

Chapter X
The Human Consciousness

31

We have conditions that need to be met before we arrive at the flourishing of our Consciousness.

Consciousness is the most elegant, effective, intelligent, and evolutionary phenomenon that a human being can experience.

One should first become evolved, perceptive, creative, healthy, aware, conscious, developed, and more human to live through consciousness.

Living through consciousness is the highest and most evolved way of existing for a human being.

Consciousness allows us to experience life for what life is with all its traits and domains. Just like perception, consciousness is not a phenomena that needs explanation but experiencing.

Vocabulary and most man's creations are not a result of consciousness; thus, there is no possible meaning to be ascribed. If we should know what it is, we should experience it. But, just like happiness, don't seek it either, for it will not just show up.

That human beings become conscious and live through consciousness is the only true solution to all humanity's problems. The only problem for humanity is that it is composed of humans and it takes time for humans to see and recognize their flaws. So, this conundrum is a hard nut to crack.

Conclusion

Each species that has walked upon Earth has had a rising time and an end of dawning. We won't be the exception to this rule.

Human beings for over 200,000 have had the grip of evolution and advancement to their benefit.

We have arisen from land animals and evolved to walk on our two feet. We walk, we run, we laugh, we speak, we think, we love. And we do all of these we great attention and joy. No other species have reached the level of enjoyment our faculties confer us. No other species can realize the myriad of creations we realize in our passing through this planet. Yet, we are a long way from appreciating ourselves and all the evolution that has come before us.

We are taking this land, our lives, and what surrounds us for granted.

If we begin to appreciate more our existence and the existence of all else and if we live and practice union, our experience of life and the enjoyment of being alive will take precedence over our lack of reverence and respect for ourselves.

The point of life is not to live immersed in suffering and deprivation but to flourish and exude beauty. Flowers don't know their beauty and fragrance and yet they surprise us each day with such. Why can't we also surprise others each day with our peace, our joy, our respect, our love, and compassion? Why do we need to compete amongst ourselves when just as flowers we all have a unique beauty to give and intelligence to share? It begs that we take notice of nature and how creation works and simulate it for our own benefit. There is no point in coming to experience birth and living half dead and half alive. To come here to take some space is best to enjoy the outer space that is larger and less crowded.

If we don't allow our humanity and intelligence to flourish, we will continue taking advantage of each other just like predators do.

It should be mandated to demonstrate how human and compassionate we are before even taking certain public positions so that our leaders truly work for us and not against us.

Humanity needs to improve the way it conducts itself and the way it is taking civilization forward into the future.

Today's technological advances are not the Eden it represents to be, and we have fallen out of the tree and cannot see the snake. We have become very weary and fearful of what serves us well and very open and courageous to try what is not there for our good. The internet and online platforms are not a replacement for the people around us and for the real world.

The water that we drink, the air that we breathe, the sun that gives us light, and the soil that sustains us are the true miracles of our existence, not the internet and all its derivatives.

It is not the first time a whole civilization succumbs to its death whether they lived in the land or in the water.

We don't know exactly what happened to those earlier civilizations, but when we ourselves succumb, those coming after won't know either what happened to us.

History can repeat itself and we need human beings with great light to help us brighten up the future of humanity. We should not forget that behind each act of neglect and human damage, there is a hand that can be brought to justice. Being complacent does not save us from disaster. Any human wrongdoings need to be brought to justice so that life can be relished once more.

My book, *It is not about Love*, is meant to make us think about life and about our humanity. This book should open us to the possibility of being more loving, more joyful, more sensible, and more caring. Moreover, we are all equal under the Sun.

It is not about Love; it is about the humanity within.